Discard

Pissard.

UNSOLVED MYSTERIES

the secret files

Bigfoot

Greg Cox

the rosen publishing group's
**rosen
central**

Dedicated to Sasquatch, wherever he is

Published in 2002 by The Rosen Publishing Group, Inc.
29 East 21st Street, New York, NY 10010

First Edition

Library of Congress Cataloging-in-Publication Data

Cox, Greg, 1959–
Bigfoot / by Greg Cox.— 1st ed
p. cm. — (Unsolved mysteries)
Includes bibliographical references.
Summary: Discusses the possible existence, sightings, and captures of the creature known as Bigfoot.
ISBN 0-8239-3561-2
1. Sasquatch—Juvenile literature. [1. Sasquatch.] I. Title. II. Unsolved mysteries (Rosen Publishing Group)
QL89.2.S2 C69 2001
001.944—dc21

2001003886

Manufactured in the United States of America

Contents

Stories of Bigfoot encounters have convinced many of the existence of the beast-man, despite a lack of scientific evidence.

1

A Stranger in the Forest

There you are, fishing or hiking somewhere in the evergreen forests of the Pacific Northwest, when suddenly it emerges from the bushes: a large, apelike creature, more than seven feet tall, covered from head to toe with dark black hair or fur. The monster walks upright like a person, its massive arms swinging at its sides. You know at once that this is no bear, nor even an escaped gorilla, but something far more human than either, like some sort of missing link between man and ape.

Its face is dark and hairless, with a flattened nose, and bony ridges jut out above its brown eyes. Thick black hair covers its ears, and its mouth is little more than a thin slit on the bottom half of its face. A strong animal odor, like an unwashed cage at the zoo, emanates from the beast-man, but—to your great relief—no ferocious growl or snarl reaches your ears. Instead the creature maintains an eerie silence as it watches you from only a few yards away—which is far too close for comfort!

You don't wait to see what the strange, shaggy giant does next. Both frightened and excited, you run back to your campsite, eager to tell your friends or family what you have seen. But by the time you return to the scene of your bizarre encounter, the gargantuan creature is gone. All that remains are a set of enormous footprints, pressed deeply into the dirt and mud. To your amazement, you realize that each print is over two feet long!

Native American legends and folklore have long told of wild, hairy giants living deep in the forests of North America. Tales of American and Canadian frontier encounters with such creatures date back to at least the nineteenth century. Also known as Sasquatch, a name derived from similar terms used by a variety of Canadian Indian tribes, "Bigfoot" is an ongoing mystery, with new sightings being reported—and new tracks being discovered—on a regular basis.

Does an entire species of giant primates, unrecognized by modern science, prowl the dense woodlands of the northwest United States and Canada? Hundreds of eyewitness accounts, along with much convincing physical evidence, suggest that

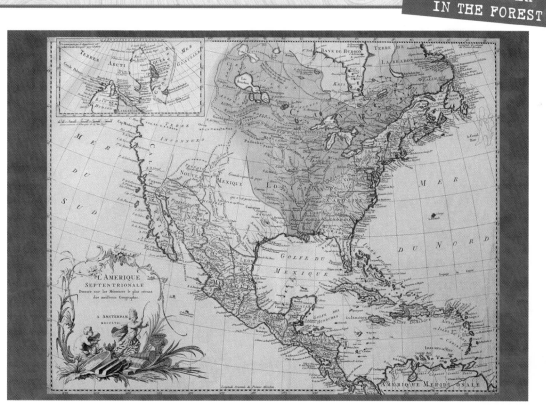

"Bigfoot" has been sighted in the forests of Canada and the northwestern United States.

something is out there in the wilderness, unseen by human civilization except for occasional chance encounters. Some people have also heard a high-pitched screeching in the night that many believe to be the distinctive cry of the Sasquatch.

Bigfoot is typically described as a large, heavy anthropoid, anywhere from seven to ten feet tall. Broad-shouldered, with a wide torso and very short neck, an adult Bigfoot may weigh as much as

800 or 900 pounds, judging from the depths to which the enigmatic footprints sink. Aside from their faces, hands, and feet, their bodies are almost completely carpeted with thick hair or fur. They appear to wear no clothing and possess no tools or other artifacts, aside from simple stones that they sometimes hurl at humans.

Bigfoot hair is usually black or reddish-brown, although there were several sightings of a white-haired Bigfoot back in the 1950s and 1960s. Possibly this was a single specimen of an albino Sasquatch that has since died. Dr. Grover Krantz of Washington State University, one of the few qualified scientists to make a serious study of the subject, estimates that the average lifespan of a Bigfoot is about forty years, which would certainly explain the disappearance of the rare white Bigfoot.

Some Native American legends describe Sasquatches as fierce man-eaters, but this seems more folklore than fact. According to witnesses, Bigfoot has a wide and varied diet, including wild berries, nuts, roots, pine needles, and the occasional rodent or rabbit. He's also been seen digging for clams, stripping the leaves from willow bushes, and wading into cold mountain streams in search of salmon. In addition, he's sometimes been accused of stealing fish, chickens, and fresh fruit from campsites, as well as from isolated farms and residences. Some experts believe that Bigfoot is also capable of snaring wild deer and elk with his bare hands, but the evidence for this is sketchier.

Unlike all other current primates, Bigfoot is bipedal, meaning that he walks erect on two legs, much like a human being. If Bigfoot indeed exists, this means Bigfoot could probably teach us a lot about the evolution of the human species. At present, most scientists believe that homo sapiens (that is, us) are the only bipedal hominids to walk the earth, and have been the only ones ever since our prehistoric cousins, the Neanderthals, died off 30,000 years ago. But what if the scientists are wrong and we still share our planet with some kind of primitive ape-man?

The prospect of accidentally running into a nonhuman creature over seven feet tall is a frightening one, but how dangerous is Bigfoot? In most modern instances, Bigfoot appears more interested in avoiding humans than in attacking them, but there are older stories in which the Sasquatch behaves much more aggressively. A Canadian prospector named Albert Ostman repeatedly claimed to have been abducted and temporarily held hostage by an entire family of Sasquatches—a father, a mother, and two young children—back in 1924. Trapped in a remote valley somewhere in British Columbia, Canada, he spent a couple of days observing the creatures, who mostly left him alone. Ostman finally managed to escape by tricking the large male Bigfoot into trying some of his powdered tobacco. The noxious snuff made the creature so violently ill that Ostman was able to flee the valley during the confusion. Why did the father Sasquatch kidnap the prospector in the first place? Perhaps it was simple curiosity. Or maybe he was more interested in Ostman's gear and provisions.

The very same year, on Mount St. Helens in Washington State, another set of prospectors claim to have fought off a hostile band of enraged Bigfoots after the men shot (and possibly killed) a large, gorilla-like creature in what is now called Ape Canyon. The prospectors' log cabin was besieged at night by apelike "mountain devils" who shrieked and howled as they hurled heavy rocks at the walls and roof of the cabin. At one point during that terrifying evening, a hairy arm invaded the cabin through a chink in the wall, groping for an axe, before being repelled by gunfire. The frightened miners later described their attackers as having "the appearance of huge gorillas," their massive bodies covered all over with long black hair. They also found numerous footprints, roughly two feet in length.

It is worth noting that the name "Bigfoot" was not coined until 1958, over three decades after the Ape Canyon incident. The whole notion of an unknown man-monster running around the Northwest did not really become widespread until national newspapers started covering the topic in the late fifties. Nevertheless, a 1924 Oregon newspaper account of the prospectors' bizarre story mentions that "Indians have told of the 'mountain devils' for sixty years" and that tracks such as the miners described "have been seen by forest rangers and prospectors for years." In other words, Bigfoot was haunting the forests long before he became famous.

In 1884, according to another newspaper clipping, a strange creature, "something of a gorilla type," was captured alongside railroad tracks in British Columbia. The hairy monster, nicknamed "Jacko," was apparently spying on a passenger train when people aboard the train spotted him. The train was stopped so that they could chase after the creature. They eventually knocked Jacko unconscious with a rock, tied him up with a heavy rope, then shipped him to the nearby town of Yale. What happened next is a

An 1884 sighting of a huge hairy beast by train travelers brought reports of its capture. No further records exist.

mystery. Much to the extreme frustration of Bigfoot researchers, who have spent countless hours poring through old newspapers looking for more information about this incident, no record remains of what eventually happened to Jacko. Most likely, he died in captivity not long after being caught, which would account for the puzzling lack of follow-up stories.

Judging from the description in the original report, Jacko sounds like a young Sasquatch, not yet fully grown. He was four feet seven inches tall, approximately 127 pounds, and "resembles a human being with one exception, his entire body, excepting his hands (or paws) and feet are covered with glossy hair about one inch long." Apparently unable to speak, Jacko only barked and growled at his captors.

Some skeptics have questioned whether the Jacko incident actually happened. If the *Victoria Daily Colonist* is to be believed, however, it remains the only documented account of a Bigfoot being captured alive.

No less a person than former U.S. president Theodore Roosevelt provided a secondhand account of an unusually violent Bigfoot encounter said to have occurred in a remote corner of Idaho sometime in the mid-1800s. In his book, *The Wilderness Hunter,* first published in 1892, Roosevelt told of a young fur trapper whom, after being stalked for a day or two by a smelly, two-legged creature, returned to his camp one evening to find his trapping partner dead, his neck broken. Wrote Roosevelt, "The footprints of the unknown beast-creature, printed deep in the soft soil, told the whole story . . . "

Such blood-curdling adventures are unheard of today. They lead one to wonder whether Bigfoots were bolder back before civilization encroached upon their wooded domain, or if these old campfire tales simply grew more gruesome with each telling.

The Evidence

Proof of Bigfoot's existence breaks down into four basic categories: sightings, tracks, Native American myths and folklore, and one particularly tantalizing (and controversial) piece of film footage.

Bigfoot sightings, of varying degrees of reliability, have occurred all over the United States and Canada, but they are primarily concentrated in northern California, Washington, Oregon, Alaska, and British Columbia. Mount St. Helens, site of the famous Ape Canyon incident in 1924, was once a hot spot for Sasquatch encounters, along with Bluff Creek, California, and the Blue Mountains near Walla Walla, Washington. More recently, Bigfoot hunters have concentrated their efforts on a particular region in Wyoming, located somewhere between Cody and Yellowstone National Park. In addition, the Florida Everglades may also hide a Bigfoot, or perhaps one of its relatives. (See chapter four.)

Many sightings take place at night, alongside lonely stretches of road near homes, and numerous witnesses have reported that Bigfoot's eyes reflected light like those of a cat, appearing to glow red or yellow or green. A pungent and unpleasant odor emanates from the furry creature, which is strongly recalled by almost everyone who encounters Bigfoot. Very rarely is more than one Sasquatch seen at a time, and usually only for as long as it takes the creatures to disappear back into the murky shadows of the forest. Although many determined hunters have deliberately set out in search of Bigfoot, the elusive Sasquatch has seldom been spotted on purpose. Most people who see Bigfoot do so by

Most evidence of Bigfoot has been found in the creatures' footprints left behind in soft soil.

accident, having simply been in the right place (or the wrong place, depending on their perspective) at the right time.

Over a dozen sightings are recorded every year, and it is believed that many more Bigfoot encounters go unreported because the witnesses are afraid of being ridiculed or harassed by the media. There are also unconfirmed rumors that some witnesses have been pressured to keep silent as part of a larger conspiracy to keep Bigfoot's existence a secret. (See chapter six.)

Perhaps the most persuasive evidence of Bigfoot's presence are the gigantic footprints that inspired his popular nickname. Often more than fourteen inches long, the tracks, which resemble the impression of a bare human foot, are too large and wide to belong to a human being or even a gorilla. The prints also sink much deeper than a human footprint, confirming that they were left behind by something bigger and heavier than any ordinary human. The prints are usually found in wet, soft soil, mud, or snow, and have often been discovered not far from where Bigfoot has been glimpsed. The spacing of the tracks suggest that the creature has an enormous stride, and that he can easily step over obstacles such as fences and boulders.

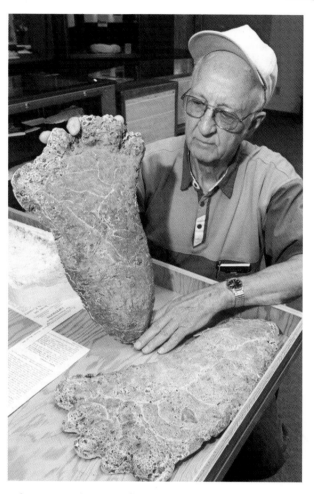

A volunteer guide at the Willow Creek-China Flat Museum in Willow Creek, California holds a plaster cast of a Bigfoot imprint on display at the museum.

Are the tracks for real? Although there have been numerous hoaxes, confusing the issue and prejudicing some people against the possibility that Sasquatches actually exist, Bigfoot experts believe that many of the giant footprints are authentic. Careful analysis of the most believable tracks reveals an astonishing degree of detail, including impressions of realistic wrinkles and ridges in the fleshy parts of the creatures' feet. Furthermore, subtle differences between human and Sasquatch footprints make sense anatomically, when you take into account Bigfoot's superior size and weight. Anyone faking these tracks would have to possess an extensive knowledge of human and ape anatomy, as well as a thorough understanding of the physics of biped locomotion. Dr. Grover Krantz, mentioned in the previous chapter, even points to one set of tracks that seems to belong to a Sasquatch with a crippled right foot, which raises the question: Why would any would-be hoaxer deliberately manufacture a deformed Bigfoot's tracks?

Although footprints are the most common type of impression left behind by Bigfoot, other kinds of tracks have occasionally been found as well. Hand and knuckle prints, possibly created when a Sasquatch stumbled and/or began to rise from a sitting position, reveal that Bigfoot's hands are also larger and wider than an adult human's hands. He also seems to lack an opposable thumb, something confirmed by a number of eyewitness reports.

In addition, a recent expedition into the Gifford Pinchot National Forest in southern Washington uncovered what appeared to be the impression of Bigfoot's butt! To be more specific, an expert team from the Bigfoot Field Researchers Organization found the clear imprint of a Sasquatch's "left forearm, hip, thigh, and heel" in a muddy stretch of ground where the researchers had left apples as bait the evening before. (Check out www.bfro.net for a full report—and pictures—of this extraordinary discovery.)

The indigenous peoples of North America, called Native Americans in the United States and First Nation Canadians above the border, have known of Bigfoot for many generations. The myths and folklore of numerous Northwest Native American tribes describe large, smelly, hairy giants who dwell in the hills and forests, apart from humanity. These creatures go by many names—Sesquac, Seatco, tsiatko, dsonqua, sokquatl, and more—but often bear a striking resemblance to the popular conception of Bigfoot. Although many of these stories give Bigfoot supernatural traits and powers, this doesn't mean that they should be dismissed entirely on scientific grounds. After all, Native Americans and First Nation Canadians tell similar stories about bears and ravens and other real-life animals, and no one says that bears and ravens only exist in myths!

Bigfoot-like creatures can also be found on totem poles, pottery, and other Indian artifacts. Particularly intriguing are several prehistoric stone heads that were found along the shores of the Columbia River, between Oregon and Washington State. Although little is known about the people who carved these heads hundreds

This blurred image of an oversized, hairy creature that walks upright is the best
available photographic evidence that Bigfoot exists.

of years ago, the chiseled stones feature distinctly apelike faces, even though ancient Northwest Indians would have had no knowledge of any primate except man. With no exposure to chimps or gorillas or even monkeys, whom could these forgotten sculptors have been trying to depict except Sasquatch?

Perhaps the most famous piece of evidence, aside from all those oversized footprints, is 952 frames of color film footage shot by a man named Roger Patterson in Bluff Creek, California, in October 1967. The footage appears to show a full-grown Sasquatch striding confidently along a sunlit creek bed littered with fallen timber and other debris from the stream. At one point, the Bigfoot, which is coated with dark black fur, looks back at the viewer before walking farther away, at which point the camera ran out of film.

Bigfoot tracks had often been found in that region of northern California, including some discovered earlier that summer. Patterson and his friend, Bob Gimlin, had been searching for Bigfoot on horseback when they supposedly stumbled onto the creature at Bluff Creek. Later, after losing track of the immense black figure in the woods, Patterson and

Gimlin made casts of the creature's footprints, which were over two feet long. This brief snippet of film, which runs slightly less than two minutes, has been analyzed and argued about for over three decades now. Although it has frequently been dismissed as a hoax, this has never been proven, and many experts continue to vouch for its authenticity.

A persistent rumor exists that the Bigfoot in the film is actually an actor wearing a costume created by John Chambers, the famous Hollywood makeup artist who won an Academy Award for his work on the original *Planet of the Apes* movie. However, Chambers has reportedly denied any part in the incident. Furthermore, the naked Bigfoot in the Patterson film doesn't even resemble the fully clothed talking simians in the 1968 movie.

More recently, a Discovery Channel television special attempted to prove that the footage was fake by hiring Optic Nerve, a Hollywood makeup studio, to recreate the film, but this argument ignores the fact that the Patterson film, if it was faked, was taken by amateurs way back in 1967. The fact that a team of professional monster-makers, employing modern, state-of-the-art makeup techniques, was able to build a convincing Bigfoot hardly proves that a couple of cowboys like Patterson and Gimlin were able to do the same in the late sixties!

It's even more ridiculous to imagine that, if it was just a hoax, the two men were not in on it. Since both men were armed with rifles, anyone trying to trick them by parading around in a homemade ape suit was taking a tremendous risk. What if either man had taken a shot at the apparent Bigfoot? Furthermore, why go to the enormous trouble and expense of pulling off the hoax if you're not going to share in the money made from the resulting film?

In over thirty years, no one has ever come forward to take credit for the hoax. Patterson stood by his story until he died in 1972, and Gimlin has never wavered either, even though he has never profited personally from the film. If the famous Patterson film is indeed genuine, as most serious Bigfoot researchers believe, then this precious footage provides us with our best glimpse yet of what Bigfoot truly looks like.

What Is Bigfoot?

Unlike, say, ghosts or fairies, there is nothing in modern science that precludes the existence of creatures such as Bigfoot. We already know that gorillas, chimpanzees, gibbons, and orangutans inhabit Earth. In biology, these advanced primates are called hominoids, a category that also includes humans (homo sapiens). At one time, the African mountain gorilla was regarded as a myth, until science proved otherwise. Why shouldn't there be large, hairy hominoids in North America as well?

Additionally, fossil records prove that all sorts of man-sized primates have existed in the past, many of them even more humanlike than the great apes of today. Scientists keep digging up the remains of different types of early humans, some of them over four million years old. These are the hominids, a biological family that includes modern human beings as well as all of our supposedly extinct human ancestors. Throughout prehistory, at least fourteen different varieties

Some experts agree that a hominid ancestor we had thought extinct might be the modern-day Bigfoot.

of hominid have roamed free; homo sapiens has only had the world to itself for the last 30,000 years.

Or have we? Some experts believe that we have already met Bigfoot in the fossil record, that the mystery monster is actually one of our prehistoric cousins, not really extinct after all. A prime candidate is *Gigantopithecus blacki,* an ancient primate whose jawbones and teeth have been found in both China and Vietnam. As its name suggests, *Gigantopithecus* was as huge as a Bigfoot and fits the standard description of a Sasquatch. This towering creature was the largest primate to ever dwell upon Earth. It may have been as much as ten feet tall, and is believed by some authorities to have walked erect on two legs, just like Bigfoot does. *Gigantopithecus* lived as recently as 500,000 years ago. It survived

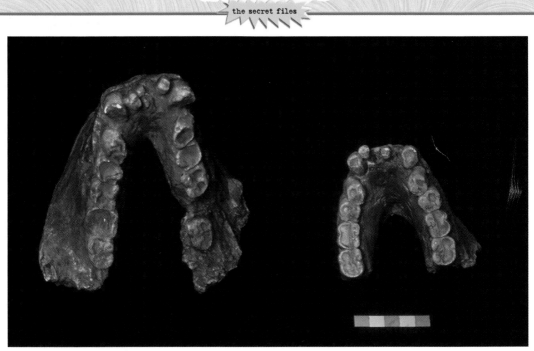

Fossilized *Gigantopithecus* jawbones found in a Chinese cave.

into the Pliocene ice age, when a land bridge connected Siberia to Alaska, allowing it to emigrate from Asia to North America, where perhaps its descendants still live today. If nothing else, the indisputable fact that *Gigantopithecus* once existed alongside our own primitive ancestors proves that a creature like Bigfoot is more than possible.

A competing theory holds that Bigfoot is some species of *Paranthropus,* a variety of ape-man believed to have lived in Africa less than two million years ago. *Paranthropus* had a bony ridge (called a sagittal crest) running along the top of its skull. The Bigfoot in the Patterson film also has such a crest, giving its head a pointed appearance, and various witnesses have also described Bigfoot's head as somewhat conical. *Paranthropus* was considerably smaller than *Gigantopithecus,* but much more human, too. In fact, it was even closer to human than a chimpanzee, our nearest living relative. It had a hairy, stocky body with longish arms, and definitely walked erect, like a human or a Sasquatch, whereas some scientists believe that *Gigantopithecus* may have been more of a knuckle-walker, like a gorilla or orangutan. Neither *Gigantopithecus,* nor *Paranthropus,* nor Bigfoot are known to have employed tools or fire, placing them at roughly the same level of cultural development.

A case can be made for either *Gigantopithecus* or *Paranthropus* being Bigfoot's true identity, but it is also possible that there is more than one kind of unknown hominid or hominoid roaming North America. Maybe both creatures still lurk in the primeval forests. Or perhaps Bigfoot is an entirely new species unknown to science. The answer remains hidden somewhere in the wilderness, beyond our present knowledge.

Bigfoot's Cousins

Bigfoot is not the only mysterious anthropoid reputed to prowl the earth. Sightings and evidence of shaggy wild men and man-apes occur all over the world, in almost every culture and country.

Beyond a doubt, Bigfoot's most famous relative is the Yeti, also known as the Abominable Snowman. Said to live in the snowy peaks of the Himalaya Mountains, on the other side of the world, the Yeti is occasionally glimpsed by explorers and mountain climbers attempting to scale Mount Everest or one of the other surrounding peaks. Its bare footprints have also been discovered from time to time, sunken deep into the stark white snow.

Like Bigfoot, the Yeti is well known to the people of Tibet and Nepal, and has deep roots in the local religion and folklore. In fact, the name "Yeti" comes from the Sherpa term *yet-teh,* which can be loosely translated to "that thing." The mountain-dwelling monster did not become world famous, however, until 1921, when a British expedition to Mount Everest spotted dimly seen figures moving about high upon the mountain slopes, where the explorers later found a set of large, unexplained footprints. A Calcutta, India, newspaper reported the incident, referring to the unknown creature as the Abominable Snowman. This was nothing more than a mistranslation of another Sherpa phrase, which actually meant something like "man-sized snow creature," but the more colorful name quickly caught on with the public, and the story of the Abominable Snowman soon spread across the planet.

Since then, several expeditions have set out in search of the Yeti, while others have attempted (unsuccessfully) to debunk the legend. One popular theory holds that the Yeti do not actually live in the mountains, but in the secluded jungle valleys between the peaks, only occasionally crossing the frozen slopes

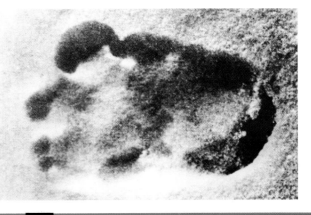

Yeti snowtracks, resembling that of a huge humanlike foot, have been found in the Himalaya Mountains.

to get from one valley to another. So far nothing has been proven either way, although mountaineers continue to spot a mysterious figure amidst the endless snow, or else find inexplicable tracks high in the mountains.

The Yeti and Sasquatch are closely linked in the public imagination. In fact, Bigfoot has often been described as the Abominable Snowman of America. Aside from the fact that they both leave puzzling footprints behind, however, there is no strong reason to assume that they belong to the same species of unknown hominoid. Although the Yeti is rarely seen close up (and eyewitness reports vary) in general, the mountain creature sounds smaller than the average Bigfoot. Some researchers believe that the Yeti is closer to an orangutan than a Sasquatch, although it is impossible to know for sure. Since the forbidding peaks of the Himalayas are even harder and more dangerous to explore than the densest North American forests, the mystery of the Abominable Snowman is not likely to be solved anytime soon.

Closer to home, the Florida Skunk Ape may or may not be a separate and distinct breed of Bigfoot found in the Florida Keys and Everglades. Like the Sasquatch of the Pacific Northwest, the Skunk

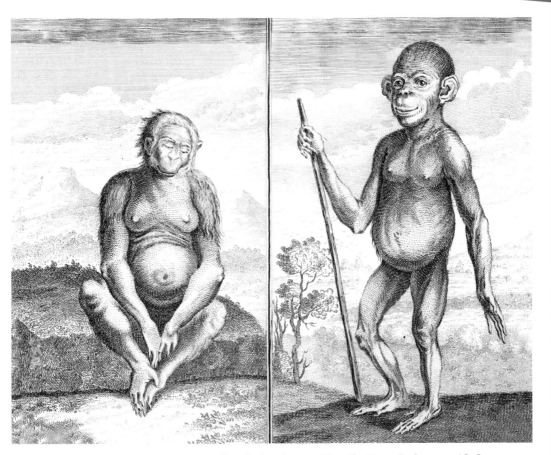

People who claimed to have seen the Skunk Ape in the Florida Everglades provided descriptions that resemble primates captured in Angola and taken to Europe around 1800.

Ape is a smelly, apelike creature whose actual existence remains not only unproved but also unacknowledged by modern science. The Skunk Ape, whose strong and unpleasant odor has offended the nostrils of just about every witness who ever encountered the semi-mythical creature, first gained widespread notoriety during the

1970s, although there are scattered accounts of its presence dating back much further.

Is the Skunk Ape simply a southern variety of Bigfoot, or a different kind of anthropoid altogether? That depends on whom you talk to. Some reports describe a tall, bipedal primate much like a traditional Sasquatch—whom, it should be recalled, is also usually described as being extremely foul smelling. Other sightings, however, seem to involve a much smaller and more apelike creature, comparable to a chimpanzee or small orangutan. Some noted cryptozoologists—scientists who study possibly mythical creatures—such as Loren Coleman, author of numerous books on the subject, believe that there may well be two separate types of unknown primates lurking behind the lush foliage of the Florida Everglades.

In any case, sightings of some kind of Skunk Ape continue to this day. As recently as December 2000, two intriguing color photos were mailed anonymously to the sheriff's department in Sarasota, Florida. The eye-catching pictures capture two views of a shaggy, gray-haired creature with a silvery beard. Two red eyes reflect the glare of the flashbulbs. Although partially concealed behind a leafy shrub, the monster in the photos does look something like an adult male orangutan, especially around the face.

Could these be genuine snapshots of Florida's famous Skunk Ape? Although an investigation continues into the origins of the photos (now known as the Myakka ape photographs after the Myakka State Park in Florida) these pictures have not yet been proven to be fake. You can check out the photos for yourself at www.lorencoleman.com.

The Yeti and the Skunk Ape are only two of the most notable anthropoids believed to be hiding in the world's diverse wilderness regions. On mainland China, the mysterious yeren, a shaggy, red-haired wild man, has been the subject of extensive research and speculation. Unfortunately, when it comes to acquiring definitive proof of the yeren's existence, Chinese cryptozoologists have not had any better luck than their North American counterparts, so the true nature of the yeren remains unknown.

Meanwhile, Russian scholars speak of the almas of Mongolia, who may or may not be the last surviving remnants of our Neanderthal cousins. And down under, on the continent of Australia, there are occasional sightings of a yowie, which sounds an awful lot like a Sasquatch—except that it only has four toes on each foot! Lastly, cryptozoologists are still searching the jungles of Sumatra for the orang-pendek, a five-foot-tall, bipedal primate that stands a good chance of being photographed any day now. Even skeptics who scoff at Bigfoot and the Yeti concede that the orang-pendek probably exists.

How all these other creatures relate to Bigfoot remains to be discovered, but it is worth remembering that early humans are known to have coexisted with *Gigantopithecus,* the Neanderthals, and many other prehistoric manlike creatures. What's more, many of these manlike beings survived for millions of years before (supposedly) becoming extinct. Given that all of recorded history is far less than 50,000 years—just a tiny sliver of time in the ongoing evolution of humanity—we should not be too surprised to find out that we're not really as unique as we think we are.

To Shoot or Not to Shoot?

Suppose that you are out hunting, your rifle loaded and ready, when you run into a Sasquatch in the woods. You have the legendary creature squarely in your sights, providing a target almost too gargantuan to miss. Here's your chance to bag a Bigfoot, proving his existence once and for all. Do you squeeze the trigger?

This question sparks serious debate among Bigfoot hunters and experts. Some argue that only an actual specimen of a dead Bigfoot will convince modern science that Bigfoot is real and not just a colorful legend. Clearly, footprints, film footage, and plenty of eyewitness testimony have not been enough to silence the skeptics. Therefore it may be necessary to sacrifice the life of one Sasquatch in order to prove that they exist, and thus secure legal protection for the rest of the species.

Others insist that it would be a crime and a tragedy to murder a Bigfoot just for the sake of scientific curiosity. They would rather see

a Sasquatch captured alive, perhaps via traps or tranquilizers, or maybe just caught on film again, but more clearly than on that much-disputed Patterson film. Given time, perhaps dedicated Bigfoot hunters will accumulate enough photos and physical evidence to convince the entire scientific community that Bigfoot is no more mythical than the grizzly bear or mountain gorilla.

Is Bigfoot an endangered species? At present, there is no way to know for sure. There is no evidence that Bigfoot is being hunted to extinction. An estimated 2,000 to 5,000 Sasquatches live on the North American continent. Furthermore, Bigfoot cannot be officially declared an endangered species until mainstream science determines that he is real.

At least a few parts of the country, however, are not waiting for definitive proof of Bigfoot's existence before leaping to his defense. In 1969, the board of county commissioners of Skamania County, in southwestern Washington State, passed the first ordinance anywhere in the United States to impose legal penalties for the premeditated and wanton slaying of "a nocturnal primate mammal generally and commonly known as a 'Sasquatch,' 'Yeti,' 'Bigfoot,' or 'Giant Hairy Ape.'" Originally, Ordinance No. 69-01 deemed the killing of a Bigfoot to be a felony, punishable by a fine of not more than $10,000 and/or five years in jail. But the law was amended in 1984, downgrading the crime to a misdemeanor and reducing the maximum penalty to a $1,000 fine and/or one year in jail. (The change was made for strictly legal reasons, since it turned out that the board did not actually have the authority to impose the more severe penalties.)

The amended law (Ordinance No. 1984-2) also declared Bigfoot to be an endangered species, establishing Skamania County as a "Sasquatch Refuge." A few years later, in 1992, Whatcom County, which lies farther north than Skamania, just below the Canadian border, passed its own resolution (No. 92-043) declaring the entire county "a Sasquatch protection and refuge area."

To date, no one has ever been prosecuted for shooting a protected Sasquatch, although

Two county governments in the United States have passed laws against killing a Sasquatch.

any gun-toting Bigfoot hunter might want to think twice before going on safari in either Skamania or Whatcom Counties. Ultimately, the question of whether it is morally justifiable—or legal—to shoot a Bigfoot comes down to the unresolved matter of just how human Bigfoot really is. Is Bigfoot some sort of primitive human or just another type of ape? Hominid or hominoid?

As far as we know, Bigfoot does not use tools, has not discovered how to make fire, does not practice agriculture, possesses no tamed animals or pets, has no written language, and may even lack the power of speech. By these standards, Bigfoot is an animal and fair game for hunters until such time as he is declared a protected species.

On the other hand, homo sapiens were once mere hunter-gatherers, too, and who knows what Bigfoot's ultimate potential might be. His bipedal gait suggests that he is more closely akin to humans than either chimpanzees or gorillas, and both of those apes have been successfully taught to communicate by sign language. Bigfoot might be capable of learning so much more. Chances are, it will be the violent death of a blameless Sasquatch that finally forces us to define what "human" really means.

The Bigfoot Cover-up?

As mankind steadily encroaches upon the wilderness, how long can Bigfoot remain hidden? And why hasn't more evidence of his existence turned up?

Could there be a conspiracy at work? For years there have been rumors and whispers that powerful logging and mining interests are deliberately suppressing proof that Bigfoot is real. Such charges have never been proven, or even thoroughly investigated, but there is a certain logic to these theories.

If Bigfoot was conclusively demonstrated to exist—if a living or dead specimen was finally obtained, then large portions of his native habitat might be declared off-limits to logging, mining, drilling, and future development. In recent years, concern for such creatures as the snail darter and the spotted

Proven existence of a Sasquatch could make thousands of forested areas off-limits to loggers.

owl have slowed or halted major industrial projects. Concrete evidence that a rare, possibly endangered species of hominoid lives in North America's forests would certainly cause tremendous controversy—and force an immediate reevaluation of all sorts of logging and drilling projects. With millions of dollars and thousands of jobs at stake, is it any wonder that some Bigfoot hunters worry that powerful vested interests may be deliberately obstructing the search for Sasquatch?

There's even been speculation that unknown parties may be responsible for some of the most blatantly ridiculous hoaxes and theories, in order to discredit and discourage serious inquiry into the subject. After all, what better way to promote disbelief in Bigfoot than to hire people to manufacture obviously fake photos or footprints, or to spread crazy stories that Bigfoot is a telepathic alien from outer space?

If Bigfoot is real, however, then it is only a matter of time before the relentless press of civilization brings Bigfoot out of the shadows of the untamed wilderness and into the light. How will Bigfoot react then?

Bigfoot might just fight against civilization. If the older campfire stories are to be believed, Bigfoot was more aggressive back in the pioneer days, before he learned to fear the newcomers and their guns. Remember the attack in Ape Canyon? The trapper killed in frontier Idaho? For now, Bigfoot would rather hide than fight—but what happens when we push these secretive giants too far?

Glossary

anthropoid   A creature resembling a human, usually applied to the higher apes, such as the chimpanzee, gorilla, orangutan, and gibbon.

Bigfoot   Popular nickname for a mysterious apelike creature believed to live deep in the forests of North America. The term was first used in 1958 by *The Humboldt Times,* a small California newspaper.

biped   Any animal that walks on two feet.

cryptid   A mystery animal whose existence is not yet accepted by modern science, such as Bigfoot, the Abominable Snowman, or the Loch Ness Monster.

cryptozoology   The study of mystery animals whose existence has been reported but not yet scientifically proven.

genus   The classification of all living things according to their characteristics, into increasingly smaller and specific categories. The names for these categories, in descending order, are: kingdom, phylum, class, order, family, genus, species.

Gigantopithecus blacki   An immense prehistoric primate, possibly the largest ever, known to have lived in Asia between 500,000 and one million years ago. Often suggested as a possible ancestor of both Bigfoot and the Abominable Snowman.

hominid   Members of the biological family *Hominidae*, including all species of two-legged primates, extinct and living.

hominoid   Members of the larger superfamily *Hominoidae*, including humans, great apes, and gibbons. Not to be confused with hominid.

paranthropus   Genus of prehistoric hominids who lived in Africa somewhere between three to one million years ago, including *Paranthropus aethiopicus*, *P. boisei*, and *P. robustus*. (Note: some paleontologists lump *Paranthropus* in with another group of prehistoric hominids, *Australopithecus*, while other experts argue that they deserve a genus of their own.) Another possible ancestor of Bigfoot.

primate   A specific order of mammals with especially flexible hands and feet, each with five digits. Includes humans, apes, monkeys, and lemurs. Bigfoot, if he exists, is almost positively a primate.

sagittal crest   A bony ridge running lengthwise across the top of a skull, between the right and left halves of the skull. Exhibited by male gorillas and orangutans, as well as some female gorillas.

Sasquatch   Another name for Bigfoot, loosely derived from Sesquac and other similar-sounding Canadian Indian terms. Coined in the 1920s by a Canadian journalist, J. W. Burns, to label the large, hairy giants found in the myths and folklore of First Nation Canadian tribes. Now used more or less interchangeably with "Bigfoot."

For More Information

Bigfoot Encounters
http://www.n2.net/prey/bigfoot

The Bigfoot Field Researchers Organization
http://www.bfro.net

The Bigfoot Museum
http://www.bigfootmuseum.com

Bigfoot/Sasquatch FAQ
http://home.nycap.rr.com/wwilliams/BigfootFAQ.html

The Cryptozoologist
http://lorencoleman.com

International Society of Cryptozoology
http://www.izoo.org/isc

Western Bigfoot Society
http://members.tripod.com/~raycrowe

X-Project Paranormal Magazine
http://www.xproject.net

For Further Reading

BOOKS

Bader, Chris. *Strange Northwest: Weird Encounters in Alaska, British Columbia, Idaho, Oregon, and Washington.* Blaine, WA: Hancock House Publishers, 1995.

Coleman, Loren. *Tom Slick and the Search for the Yeti.* Boston, MA: Faber and Faber, 1989.

Coleman, Loren, and Jerome Clark. *Cryptozoology A to Z: The Encyclopedia of Loch Monsters, Sasquatch, Chupacabras, and Other Authentic Mysteries of Nature.* New York: Fireside/Simon & Schuster, 1999.

Coleman, Loren, and Patrick Huyghe. *The Field Guide to Bigfoot, Yeti, and Other Mystery Primates Worldwide.* New York: Avon Books, 1999.

Gordon, David George. *Field Guide to the Sasquatch.* Seattle, WA: Sasquatch Books, 1995.

Green, John. *Encounters with Bigfoot.* Blaine, WA: Hancock House Publishers, 1980.

Green, John. *On the Track of the Sasquatch.* Blaine, WA: Hancock House Publishers, 1995.

Krantz, Grover S. *Bigfoot Sasquatch Evidence.* Blaine, WA: Hancock House Publishers, 1999.

Messner, Reinhold. *My Quest for the Yeti: Confronting the Himalayas' Deepest Mystery.* Translated by Peter Constantine. New York: St. Martin's Press, 2000.

Pyle, Robert Michael. *Where Bigfoot Walks: Crossing the Dark Divide.* Boston, MA: Houghton Mifflin, 1995.

ARTICLES

Begley, Sharon with Lara Santoro. "The New Old Man." *Newsweek,* April 2, 2001, pp. 46–47.

Coleman, Loren. "The Myakka Skunk Ape Photographs." *Fate,* May 2001, pp. 8–11.

Lemonick, Michael D., and Andrea Dorfman. "Up From the Apes." *Time,* August 23, 1999, pp. 50–58.

Index

ABOUT THE AUTHOR

Greg Cox grew up in Bigfoot country—the Pacific Northwest. He is the author of numerous books based on such television series as *Star Trek, Roswell,* and *Xena: Warrior Princess*. He lives in Oxford, Pennsylvania.

PHOTO CREDITS

Cover © Corbis; p. 4 by Thomas Forget; p. 7 © Corbis Royalty Free; p. 12 © *The Herald*/AP Wide World; pp. 15, 20, 29 © Bettmann/Corbis; p. 17 © AP Wide World; p. 25 © *National Geographic*; p. 26 © Forrest Anderson/Time Pix; p. 31 © Hulton/Archive by Getty Images; p. 37 © Russell Illig/Photodisc; p. 40 © *Alexandria Daily Town Talk*/AP Wide World.

SERIES DESIGN AND LAYOUT

Geri Giordano